THE "HOW-TO" GUIDE ON BECOMING A CERTIFIED NURSING ASSISTANT

Find a School
Pay for Training
Prepare for the Exam
Get a Job
Jump-start Your Career

SHEILAH MARA
&
TERRY B. THOMAS

COPYRIGHT

lines change and it is the reader's responsibility to be aware of these changes and of the policies and procedures of his or her own healthcare facility or training facility or institution. The reader should stay informed of any new changes or recommendations made by federal, state, and local agencies. The authors do not warrant or guarantee any of the products described herein. Adherence to all applicable laws and regulations, including international, federal, state, and local governing professional licensing, business practices, advertising, and all other aspects of doing business in the US, Canada, or any other jurisdiction is the sole responsibility of the purchaser or reader.

Neither the author nor the publisher assumes any responsibility or liability whatsoever on the behalf of the purchaser or reader of these materials. Any perceived slight of any individual or organization is purely unintentional.

CONTENTS

Introduction

HOW THIS BOOK CAN HELP YOU

You want to know —

How do I jump-start my career in healthcare?

How do I become a Certified Nursing Assistant?

Where can I find training, and can I afford it?

Where do I begin?

If you are thinking about becoming a Certified Nursing Assistant, or CNA, you are probably searching for answers to your most basic questions, and your search has brought you here. Whether it is a calling or an impulse, this book is for you. It contains essential information for the aspiring CNA.

The chapters in this book will help guide you along your career path as a CNA. Although the primary focus is long-term care, the information and resources are applicable to any healthcare setting where CNAs are employed.

You will learn what a CNA does and how this occupation differs from other similar jobs in the healthcare sector. You also will learn how to select a training program, what to expect, whether you meet eligibility requirements, and ways to pay for training (and even get it free). In addition, you will learn about the competency exam and get tips on how to prepare.

We offer advice on how to land a job after you have passed the exam, and how to keep it. We also discuss professional development as well as current and emerging trends in the workplace so you can start your career as a CNA on a solid foundation.

If you are new to the field of healthcare, our self-assessment will help you determine how well your personal attributes align with career CNAs. We also acquaint you with the tasks and responsibilities CNAs encounter on a daily basis, as well as the tools of their trade. Whether you are in high school, a single parent, seeking a career change — or just starting one, you will find information and resources throughout this book that will be helpful to you.

The organization of this book consists of short chapters, Quick Facts, and additional resources. Our *Quick Facts* section, presented at the end of selected chapters, imparts important terms and concepts that we think you should know. When you see a term or phrase highlighted in ***bold and italics*** in the chapters, you will find additional information in *Quick Facts*. Also, because requirements for CNAs vary by state, we've included links to each state, U.S. territories and the District of Columbia at the end of the book.

Our combined experience totals more than 40 years in the field of healthcare and long-term care, which includes direct patient/resident care, training and supervision, quality assurance, and executive leadership. Our theoretical knowledge, clinical and practical experience, and collaborations with our skilled colleagues in the field have been essential in the development of this book, and we are excited to share what we know.

Should you decide that becoming a CNA is the right career path for you, this book can be your roadmap to a less frustrating and more satisfying journey toward your goal, and hopefully, a long-term career in healthcare.

So congratulations on taking this first step. Let's get started!

Chapter 1

THE EVER-RISING DEMAND FOR CERTIFIED NURSING ASSISTANTS

It is no surprise the demand for Certified Nursing Assistants (CNAs) is enormous and growing. For the next 20 years, roughly 9,000 Americans will turn 65 every day. By 2030, there will be more than 71 million people over the age of 65. Those 85 and over are becoming the fastest-growing segment among the elderly, and more people are living to age 100 and beyond. In fact, the population of centenarians has doubled in the past 30 years, according to the U.S. Census Bureau.

Baby Boomers (individuals born in the U.S. between 1946 and 1964) are living longer and healthier than any generation before them, and they intend on enjoying an active and independent lifestyle well into an advanced age. However, at some point, they will need assistance, whether from a family member or by a professional caregiver, such as a CNA.

Nationally, there are approximately 1,500,000 active CNAs. About one-third provide services to nearly two million *residents* living in *long-term care facilities (LTCFs),* or nursing homes. However, as impressive as their numbers are, and even with the anticipated surge in this occupation in the next 15 years, some areas across the country are anticipating a shortfall of these healthcare providers.

Without doubt, CNAs are essential to the healthcare industry, and this is especially true in long-term care settings. In an LTCF, they provide daily routine assistance with basic tasks residents may not be able to do on their own (commonly known as *Activities of Daily Living or ADLs)*, as well as social, psychological, and spiritual support.

Working under the supervision of a licensed nurse, they are a critical member of the healthcare team. CNAs often are viewed as "front-line workers" and the "eyes and ears" of the team because they have the most frequent contact with residents among all of the healthcare providers. Because of this high degree of interaction, they can relay important information regarding any change in a resident's behavior and condition. We like to refer to them as the "first responders."

In the next chapter, we will take a look at why certification is essential for CNAs.

Quick Facts

1. **Long-term care (LTC)** refers to a range of 24-hour services (both medical and nonmedical) provided to the elderly and persons with a chronic illness or disability. Traditionally, long-term care has been associated with nursing homes and skilled nursing facilities (where medi-

cal care is required). But today, it can also refer to care that is provided in assisted-living facilities and in the home.

2. **LTCF** is the acronym for *long-term care facility.*

3. **A resident** "resides" in a long-term care facility such as a nursing home or assisted living facility, and has a permanent address and phone number at the establishment. In contrast, a *patient* receives care in a hospital setting or medical center, while those who receive services in the home are *clients.* Because this book focuses on long-term care, you will encounter the term *resident* more frequently than "patient" or "client." However, this book is applicable to CNAs who want to work in any setting.

4. **Activities of Daily Living (ADLs)** are tasks an individual can perform on a daily basis without assistance: walking, eating, dressing, bathing, transferring (e.g., from bed to chair), grooming (hair and teeth), and using the toilet.

Chapter 2

WHY CERTIFICATION IS IMPORTANT

Prior to the late 1980s, nurse assistants did not have to be certified. So why is it important today?

In 1987, President Reagan signed into law the Omnibus Budget Reconciliation Act (OBRA). OBRA changed how long-term care facilities provided services to residents by establishing standards of quality care, and minimum training standards for those providing care. Before OBRA came into effect, there were growing concerns from the public that nursing homes were not providing proper care to residents. With the passage of OBRA, any LTCF receiving payments from *Medicare* and *Medicaid* programs must comply with OBRA laws and regulations.

The Nursing Home Reform Act, which is a part of OBRA, specifies what types of services LTCFs have to provide to their residents. The law affirms that residents have the same basic rights afforded to everyone else in the larger community. These rights are often referred to the "Residents' Bill of Rights." Facilities are mandated to protect and promote the rights of residents and to ensure that these rights are not violated. LTCFs are also required to maintain a resident's quality of life, maintain their dignity and promote self-determination.

To view a list of these rights see https://www.medicare.gov/ NursingHomeCompare/Resources/Resident-Rights.html

Or use this shortened URL: http://bit.ly/2bhiv2R

In order to implement this mandate, training and education standards were established, including those for *Nurse Aides*. Under the Nurse Aide Training and Competency and Evaluation Program (NATCEP), each state is allowed to implement a training program, as long as it consists of at least 75-hours of instruction and skills training.

In addition to required training, Nurse Aides must pass a competency examination consisting of the following components:

1. Basic nursing skills
2. Personal care skills
3. Basic restorative skills
4. Mental health and social service skills
5. Caring for cognitively impaired resident
6. Resident's rights

After passing the competency examination, OBRA requires that CNAs must be registered by the state in order to work in an LTCF. To remain certified and active in the registry, CNAs must complete annual ***in-service*** training. We will discuss the state registry and other requirements in more detail in the coming chapters.

While there have been occasional revisions and updates, OBRA is getting overhauled to incorporate contemporary standards of practice.

In the next chapter, we take a look at the various job titles of CNAs and discuss similar occupations providing basic levels of care.

QUICK FACTS

1. ***Medicare*** is the federal government health insurance program for people who are 65 years or older, or certain younger individuals with disabilities. ***Medicaid*** is a joint federal and state program that assists with medical costs for people with limited income and resources.

2. In long-term care facilities, and specifically nursing homes that receive Medicare and Medicaid funding, you will hear the term OBRA (or OBRA-87) in reference to all parts of the legislation pertaining to nursing home reform.

3. The term **Nurse Aide** is the original occupational description of Nursing Assistants in the OBRA legislation.

4. In this book, *Certified Nursing Assistant* and *Certified Nurse Aide* are used interchangeably, and a "nurse aide" or "nurse assistant" is one who is not yet certified. However, when referencing OBRA, Nurse Aide is capitalized.

5. **In-service** training refers to an ongoing educational, staff development program. Instruction and training are provided to employees in a group setting aimed at enhancing or expanding their skills and abilities.

Chapter 3

THE MANY FACES OF THE CNA — DIVERSITY OF JOB TITLES

Today, CNAs are known by a variety of job titles. Let's review some of them:

- Certified Nurse Aide (CNA)
- Certified Nurse's Aide (CNA)
- Certified Nursing Assistant (CNA)
- Geriatric Nursing Assistant (GNA)
- Pediatric Nursing Assistant (PNA)
- Licensed Nursing Assistant (LNA)
- Medicaid Nurse Aide
- Nurses' Aide
- Nursing Aide
- Nursing Assistant
- Patient Care Assistant/Associate
- State Tested Nursing Assistant (STNA)

- State Registered Nurse Aide
- Advanced Nurse Aide
- Advanced Certified Nurse Aide

Your specific job title will depend on where you live. Also, some job titles require additional training and experience or a credential.

While the vast majority of CNA training programs will prepare you for an entry-level position in an LTCF, there are a few exceptions. In the state of Maryland, for example, providing care to the elderly is considered a specialty, so you must earn a credential as a Geriatric Nursing Assistant (GNA) in order to work in an LTCF.

If specialties are offered in your training program, you may be able to pursue a credential while you are training as a CNA.

If you do not want to pursue a specialization at that time or the program does not offer one, there will be other opportunities for you to earn a credential. In the Commonwealth of Virginia, for example, you are eligible to become an Advanced CNA after you have gained experience as a CNA and taken additional courses.

Acquiring a credential not only increases your clinical knowledge and skills, it also may improve your job status and earnings, as well as present other opportunities for career growth. In the above example, Virginia's Advanced CNA training prepares students for entry into the practical nursing program.

Specialized training can also lead to a different job function and occupation. For example, there is specialized training to become a Certified Medication Aide, as well as a Dialysis

Technician. States that offer additional credentials for CNAs include Montana, North Carolina, Oregon, Oklahoma, and Wyoming.

Whatever title you are given to reflect your role as a CNA, you will work under the supervision of a nurse manager who is Licensed Practical Nurse (LPN) or Registered Nurse (RN).

Specific duties and responsibilities of CNAs are described further in Chapter 6.

CLOSELY RELATED OCCUPATIONS

The following occupations are often confused with the job of a CNA. Although some tasks overlap, there are significant differences in training, certification, and even supervision.

ORDERLIES

Orderlies (also known as attendants, ward assistants, patient care assistants, and sometimes, nurse assistants) help medical and/or nursing staff with various tasks, such as transporting patients to and from treatment and diagnostic areas within the hospital.

Like CNAs, a nurse supervises orderlies; however, orderlies do not need to be certified. Instead, they receive on-the-job training. Many employers also require orderlies to be certified in Basic Life Support so they are competent to perform CPR (Cardiopulmonary Resuscitation). Orderlies are a staple in hospitals, but less common in long-term care facilities.

MEDICAL ASSISTANTS

Medical Assistants (MAs) and Certified Medical Assistants (CMAs) are typically seen in physician offices, group practices and clinics (or in clinical areas of larger facilities). Both CNAs and medical assistants provide direct care. However, CNAs provide bedside care, whereas medical assistants may perform preparatory and sometimes front-office tasks. For example, medical assistants may check-in/check-out patients, take their weight, temperature, and blood pressure, escort them to examination rooms, give injections, and call in medication orders to the pharmacist. As far as administrative functions, they may schedule appointments, maintain patient records, and process billing and insurance claims. While CNAs are supervised by a licensed nurse, medical assistants might be supervised by an office manager or a physician, depending on the duties they perform. Unlike those in CNA training programs, Medical Assistants can earn an associate's degree.

HOME HEALTH CARE AIDES

As the job title suggests, home health care aides work in the homes of their clients. In addition to assisting clients with ADLs, home health care aides provide assistance in everyday tasks, referred to as Instrumental Activities of Daily Living (IADLs). These tasks include assisting with housework, managing money, reminding clients to take their medication, preparing and cleaning up after meals, grocery shopping, using a telephone, caring for pets, and responding to emergency alerts. Home health care aides must be certified.

PERSONAL CARE ATTENDANTS

Personal care attendants also work strictly in the client's home. They provide personal care such as bathing, dressing, and personal grooming. No formal education or certification is necessary. However, personal care attendants may be required to work under the supervision of a nurse or other health care professional.

NURSE AIDE/NURSE ASSISTANT (UNCERTIFIED)

As we stated earlier, some nurse aide/nurse assistant jobs do not require specific training and examination. Although these nurse aides may perform many of the same basic functions of CNAs, they cannot work in LTCFs that receive payments from Medicare and Medicaid. However, if they are pursuing their CNA certification, uncertified nurse assistants can work in an LTCF for up to four months.

There may be fewer job opportunities, lower earnings, and limited opportunities for career development for uncertified nurse aides. In some workplaces, they may even have a different job title so they are not confused with those who are certified.

KNOW THE DIFFERENCE

As you begin your job search, you will discover that many employers—including those that do not manage LCTFs— use OBRA certification requirements to qualify and hire nursing assistants under a variety of job titles. Although this may expand your job opportunities, thoroughly research your options to make sure you have selected the right occupation that aligns with your career objectives.

In the following chapter we take a closer look at where CNAs work.

Chapter 4

WHERE CNAS WORK

CNAs work in just about every field in healthcare. Because most facilities operate 24 hours a day, seven days a week, CNAs are present on all three shifts. They work days, evenings, weekends, and holidays and may be called upon to work additional shifts when the facility is short-staffed. Although the majority are hired as full-time employees, some work part-time and as contract workers. In the following sections we describe the various work settings where you will encounter CNAs.

Long-term Care Facilities (Nursing Homes) and Skilled Nursing Facilities. CNAs are in constant demand at LCTFs, and in skilled nursing facilities where residents require a higher degree of medical care. Also, because hospital stays have become shorter, CNAs help nurses provide sub-acute care in addition to long-term care. Many CNAs enjoy working in an LTCF because they get to know the residents and develop long-term relationships with them and their families.

Assisted Living. Assisted living provides a level of long-term care that is between independent living and residing in an LTCF. Residents are afforded some degree of independence in a home-like setting. CNAs provide varying degrees of assistance with ADLs, or with health-related problems that make performing ADLs difficult. Assisted-living facilities vary in size and type of services they provide. However, unlike nursing homes, assisted-living facilities get their revenue through private insurance or out-of-pocket payments from the residents or their families. Therefore, because these facilities do not rely on Medicare or Medicaid payments to operate, nurse assistants do not have to be certified.

Hospitals (i.e., Acute Care). Hospitals provide short-term, acute-care services for injuries and illnesses that require immediate attention. There are many specialties and departments where CNAs can work, and many opportunities to broaden their skills. Because hospital stays are shorter, many CNAs feel a sense of accomplishment and closure when patients are discharged. Good benefits, good pay, and stable work hours tend to attract many CNAs to hospitals.

Subacute Care. Subacute care is appropriate for those who do not require immediate acute-care services, but need more than those with chronic illnesses. Generally, it is the practice of serving those who need complex medical care or rehabilitation. This type of care is provided either in a hospital or in an LTCF. It is considered "transitional" care, and ends once the patient or resident has stabilized or when the treatment period has ended.

Rehabilitation Centers provide specialized services such as physical, speech, and occupational therapies. Rehabilitation services can be found in hospital settings, while others are independent service providers. After a period of rehabilitation, patients may be discharged to their home or transferred to an LTCF or an assisted-living facility.

Adult Day Care services provide social and limited healthcare services to adults who need supervised care outside the home during the day, or at certain hours of the day. Adult day-care services are appropriate for people who are not seriously ill or disabled. Typically, the staff consists of one or more social workers, an activity director, and activity aides who often are CNAs.

Mental Health Centers, or behavioral health units, employ CNAs as mental health technicians to assist nursing staff with elderly or disabled persons with serious emotional or mental illness. Others may work in an intermediate care facility for people with intellectual and developmental disabilities (ICF-DD).

Pediatric Hospitals and Facilities. Some CNAs work in the pediatric or children's unit of the hospital. There are also independent pediatric facilities which include not only children and teens, but also older adults with developmental disabilities or brain trauma.

Hospice Care is provided to individuals who have six months or less to live. The focus of care is centered around the patient's physical and emotional comfort, and support for their families.

Home Health Care, Personal Home Care, Travelling CNA. Elderly residents who prefer to remain in their homes can receive a wide range of care services. Home health care is becoming increasingly popular because it is less expensive than nursing homes and assisted-living facilities. Many home health caregivers enjoy the flexibility of selecting their shifts or setting their work hours.

Corrections (Correctional Healthcare). Correctional facilities (or prisons) might be an unlikely place to find CNAs, but they work along with nurses and other medical staff in providing care to the physically ill, physically challenged, and elderly inmates in maximum-security settings, detention facilities (jails), and halfway houses.

The next three chapters cover the unique qualities and attributes of CNAs, their duties and responsibilities, and the tools and technologies they use.

Chapter 5

ATTRIBUTES OF A CNA

As a Certified Nursing Assistant, you have a responsibility to those residents under your care. You must also maintain a professional demeanor with family members, your health-care team, and other staff at the facility. Confidence in your knowledge, skills, attitude, and temperament all play a role in shaping your success as a CNA.

There's an expression, "If you love what you do, you will never have to work a day in your life." In other words, enjoy what you do and your job will never seem like work. You will look forward to each day.

People who love working in healthcare and are successful CNAs possess specific characteristics, or attributes. Ask yourself: *Would I make a good CNA? Would I enjoy being a CNA?*

The goal of this chapter is to get you to think critically about why you believe a career as a CNA is right for you. To help you with this process, we've included a self-evaluation tool called the CNA's

Goodness of Fit Checklist. It was developed to help aspiring CNAs determine how well their attitudes, values, tolerances, and abilities align with those who are successful as CNAs.

Our checklist is not based on rigorous scientific procedures. Instead, it is the result of years of collaborations with managers, supervisors, multidisciplinary teams, and our professional relationships with CNAs. We invite you to take the self-assessment if you are new to healthcare or are on the fence about becoming a CNA. If you have prior experience in healthcare or are confident in your decision, you can skip this section and move on to Chapter 6.

If, after taking the assessment, you want to explore other professions outside of the field of healthcare, consider taking a *career interest* test. They are available at job placement centers or by reaching out to a high school guidance counselor, a vocational counselor, or an adviser at a technical or community college. Tests are available online for free; however, you will have to pay for the full version.

In the next chapter, we describe what CNAs are likely to encounter during the work day and the tools and technologies they use.

RESOURCES FOR THIS CHAPTER

U.S. Department of Labor, Employment and Training Administration, Tests and Other Assessments: Helping You Make Better Career Decisions, 2000/ Accessed: September 16, 2016, https://www.onetcenter.org/dl_files/testAsse.pdf

THE CNA GOODNESS-OF-FIT CHECKLIST

Instructions for the CNA Goodness-of-Fit Checklist: Examine the following statements. If a statement is an accurate description of your attitude or behavior and reflects who you are MOST of the time, check the "Y" column (for YES). Otherwise, check the "N" column (for NO). If using the form, check the appropriate box. If using a sheet a paper, write down the number to each statement and record your response next to it.

Which of these statements accurately describe who you are?	YES	NO
1. I enjoy helping people.		
2. I know how to express myself clearly so that people understand me.		
3. I am aware of how people react to what I say or do and why they react that way.		
4. I have compassion for the elderly, frail, sick or disabled.		
5. I am able to quickly adapt to good or bad events.		
6. I report to work in spite of bad weather, child-care, or transportation issues.		
7. I don't mind if, on occasion, I am asked to take an extra shift on short notice.		
8. I am respectful of people in positions of authority.		
9. I leave my personal problems "at the door" when I report to work.		
10. I am patient with someone who has difficulty speaking or communicating.		

Which of these statements accurately describe who you are?	YES	NO
11. I have strong opinions, but I don't try to force my opinions on others.		
12. It is easy for me to start a conversation with someone I don't know or just met.		
13. I can recognize when something is wrong or incorrect, or is about to go wrong.		
14. I work well under stressful situations, whether it's caused by people or events.		
15. I am not distracted by strong or unpleasant odors.		
16. If someone is having a bad day and tries to take it out on me, I don't let it bother me.		
17. I don't have a problem cleaning up bodily fluids (urine, vomit, or stool).		
18. I take time to listen and understand the point a person is making before I ask questions.		
19. I believe I can make a difference in peoples' lives.		
20. I understand what is written in official documents like letters, memos, policies, and procedures.		
21. I can present my ideas clearly when I write.		
22. I know how to appropriately adjust my reaction based on what others say or do.		
23. I can analyze problems and come up with a solution.		
24. I like things that are well-organized.		

Which of these statements accurately describe who you are?	YES	NO
25. I know how to investigate and identify the cause of a particular problem.		
26. I can concentrate on tasks even with noises and other interruptions.		
27. I am respectful of people whose background and experiences are different from mine.		
28. I would be comfortable cleaning up or bathing a sick or elderly person.		
29. I think about how I can be better at what I do.		
30. I get things done without being told to do them.		
31. I can teach someone how to perform a task.		
32. I work hard at improving my performance without a supervisor telling me.		
33. I am detailed-oriented.		
34. I am good at controlling my temper.		
35. I am honest and trustworthy.		
36. I have a sense of humor.		
37. I work well in a group or team.		
38. I can stand or move about for long periods of time.		
39. I can lift objects without difficulty.		

Which of these statements accurately describe who you are?	YES	NO
40. I follow work policy and procedures even when others tell me they aren't necessary.		
41. I give my full attention to someone who is speaking to me.		
42. I like the sciences like biology, physiology, or chemistry.		
43. I understand ideas and information presented to me.		
44. I won't get bored performing the same tasks every day.		
45. I am a good listener.		
46. I am good at managing my time.		
47. I'm willing to take on extra tasks, responsibilities, and challenges to get the job done.		
48. Healthcare jobs are important.		
49. I am sensitive to other peoples' feelings.		
50. I can stoop and reach without difficulty.		

Scoring and Interpretation: Your score is based on the number of "Yes" responses. Add all of the "Y" or "Yes" responses and refer to the interpretative summary below:

Your Score	Your Fit Category	Interpretative Summary
41 and above	**Very Good Fit**	Your attributes are highly aligned with career CNAs.
26-40	**Good Fit**	You share common attributes with those who work as CNAs.
25 or below	**Probable Fit**	You share some common attributes with those in healthcare, but fewer than most CNAs.

If your score fell within the Probable Fit category, do not get discouraged. It does not mean that becoming a CNA is out of your reach or that you won't be successful. You cannot pass or fail this assessment. It cannot predict how well you will do in the training program, or on your competency exam, or your ability to find employment. The goal of this tool is to help you do a little soul-searching. Bear in mind that your score depends on your willingness to respond honestly to each statement.

If being in the *Probable Fit* category still concerns you (perhaps you are a couple of points away from being in the next category), recalculate your score by using one of the following alternate scoring formats.

1. Review your "NO" statements and consider whether any of them reflect who you are SOME OF THE TIME. Change those to "YES" responses and add to your initial score.

2. For each "NO" response, ask yourself if that particular attribute is something you can work on by changing an attitude, becoming more tolerant, or strengthening a skill. Change those to YES, and then add to your initial score.

If either adjustment puts you into a new category, be sure to make note of those statements that you changed. Treat them as declarations and make an effort to apply your new attitudes and behaviors in everyday situations so that eventually they will become a part of who you are. Remember that real change occurs over time.

Chapter **6**

A Day in the Life of a CNA — Duties and Responsibilities

In this chapter, we describe the duties and responsibilities CNAs are likely to perform during the day and the tools and technologies of their trade.

Few people are fully aware of the tasks and responsibilities of a CNA. If you recently have completed high school, are uninterested in or unable to afford college, are new to the workforce, or having difficulty finding a career path, becoming a CNA might seem like an easy solution to finding gainful employment. Unfortunately, many aspiring but uninformed students later discover it is not the kind of job they enjoy or the work they want to do for a living.

Should you become a CNA, you will find that this occupation is not relegated to those simply in need of employable skills. On the contrary, becoming a CNA requires a combination of knowledge, skills, and abilities (or KSAs) to provide the best care possible.

You will become a member of a healthcare team that consists of a physician, nurse, dietician, social worker, activity therapist, and other specialists, depending on the resident's **care plan**. Because you are not licensed, your tasks will be assigned and supervised by a licensed professional, usually a nurse, and on occasion another licensed professional such as a physician. They are in your *line-of-authority*, also known as your chain-of-command. It is important that you have a clear understanding of your duties and responsibilities, and what you can and cannot do (your *scope of practice*).

DAILY TASKS AND RESPONSIBILITIES

CNAs cover a lot of ground during the day. In this section, we provide a snapshot of what their day entails. We generated a short list of tasks based on several sources, including the Occupational Information Network or *O*Net*. It should be evident that CNAs engage in a diversity of tasks, and not just for a single resident, but for a large group of residents.

If you are interested in seeing an extensive list of activities, the National Council of State Boards of Nursing (NCSBN) has published their 2014 job analysis and KSA study of activities that are performed by entry-level CNAs. They identify 113 activities and 201 KSAs. A link to this publication is at the end of this chapter.

Daily Tasks and Responsiblities Performed By CNAs

- Answer calls lights.
- Brush, comb, shampoo patient's/resident's hair.
- Mouth care: Brush and floss teeth (conscious or unconscious residents)/ denture care.
- Feed patients/residents.
- Bathe patients/residents.
- Provide perineal care.
- Provide nail care.
- Hold patients/residents to ensure proper positioning or safety.
- Assist practitioners performing medical procedures.
- Assess physical conditions of patients/residents to aid in diagnosis or treatment.
- Interview patients/residents to gather medical information.
- Explain technical medical information to patients/residents.
- Adjust positions of patients/residents on beds or tables.
- Move patients/residents to or from treatment or activity areas.
- Record vital statistics or other health information.
- Measure and record intake and output.
- Monitor patients/residents to detect health problems.
- Administer basic health-care or medical treatments.
- Administer therapy treatments to patients/residents using hands or physical treatment aids.
- Apply bandages, dressings, or splints.
- Give medications or immunizations.

- Collect biological specimens from patients/residents.
- Assist with bladder/bowel retraining.
- Dispose of biomedical waste in accordance with standards.
- Transport biological or other medical materials.
- Clean patient/resident rooms or patient-treatment rooms.
- Prepare medical instruments or equipment for use.
- Operate medical equipment.
- Stock medical or patient/resident care supplies.
- Perform post-mortem care.

Cognitive and mental health issues. Additional training or credentialing may be required for some tasks.

- Observe for early signs of inappropriate behavior, frustration, anger, and aggression.
- De-escalate a resident who is yelling, screaming or combative.
- Implement various approaches for a resident who is resisting personal care.
- Maintain a safe environment for the wandering resident.
- Implement care strategies that encourage ADLs without increasing resident anxiety.
- Use coaching techniques to help other caregivers and family members cope with the dementia process.

TOOLS OF THE TRADE

Equipment and tools are essential in completing the many functions of professional caregiving in LTCFs and other settings, as well as enhancing the quality of care. CNAs must be able to demonstrate a level of competency in their use, as well as keep abreast of the latest health-care technologies. We excerpt the list produced by *O*Net* to give you an idea of how sophisticated and complex some of these devices can be.

TOOLS AND TECHNOLOGIES USED BY CNAS

- Aerosol tents
- Arm slings
- Anti-embolism elastic stockings
- Automated external defibrillators (AED) or hard paddles
- Bedpans
- Blanket frames or lifters
- Blood pressure units/cuffs (manual and electronic)
- Canes (walking or cane accessories)
- Clinical hydraulic lifts or accessories
- Clinical trapeze traction bars
- Crutches or crutch accessories
- Computers (desktop and notebook)
- Extremities cradles (bed cradles)
- Extremity restraints
- Gait belts for rehabilitation or therapy
- Gloves (exam or non-surgical procedure gloves)

- Glucose monitors
- Gurneys or scissor lifts
- Hospital intercom
- Medical ultrasound, Doppler or pulse echo echography, bladder ultrasounds
- Multiline telephone systems
- Orthopedic splint sets
- Oxygen nasal cannulas, masks, tents, and tanks
- Oxygen therapy delivery equipment and supplies
- Patient beds or table scales
- Patient transfer boards or accessories
- Patient stabilization or fall prevention devices or accessories (protective patient restraints)
- Patient urinals
- Photocopying equipment
- Pulse oximeter units
- Safety razors
- Scales (patient floor scale)
- Shower or bath chairs or seats
- Specimen collection container
- Spirometers (accessories and supplies)
- Steam autoclaves or sterilizers
- Therapeutic cold packs/hot packs
- Urinalysis test strips
- Urinary catheterization kit
- Walkers or rollers
- Wheelchairs

More than Just Skilled Labor

Being a CNA requires an understanding of medical terminology, skill in using medical equipment, computer literacy, a keen sense of perception, patience, and compassion. Anyone who has ever cared for the sick or the elderly knows it can be a demanding job. In many ways, the role of the CNA has expanded far beyond performing routine tasks on a daily basis. Families and caregivers — daunted or overwhelmed by the challenges of cognitive decline from dementia, or a mental or substance abuse problem — are delegating those care and management responsibilities to the professional LTCF staff. As the CNA on the front line, you will meet these challenges head-on, every day, and no two days are the same. Successfully managing these issues requires additional, often specialized, knowledge and training, good-to-excellent interpersonal skills, the ability to deal with conflict and difficult behaviors, flexibility in trying and incorporating new strategies when existing ones are no longer effective, and a good deal of patience.

We said earlier that the perceptions of CNAs are changing. Still, you are likely to encounter people who see the work of CNAs as simply a form of skilled labor. These people typically lack any direct knowledge and experience in dealing with the many physical and *behavioral health* challenges in today's nursing homes and other LTCF settings. Those who have observed CNAs in action appreciate all that they do.

QUICK FACTS

1. *O*Net*, otherwise known as the "Occupational Information network," is an online, automated database sponsored by the federal government that replaced the Dictionary of Occupational Titles (DOT) as the primary source of occupational information.

2. A *Care Plan* (also known as a Plan of Care or treatment plan) consists of specific actions to be performed by healthcare team members aimed at improving the health outcomes of the resident, patient or client.

3. *Behavioral health* is a contemporary term now preferred over *mental health* and includes substance-abuse disorders.

RESOURCES FOR THIS CHAPTER

National Center for O*NET Development. 31-1014.00. *O*NET OnLine*. Accessed: September 16, 2016.
http://www.onetonline.org/link/summary/31-1014.00

National Center for O*NET Development. 311012.00. *O*Net Online*. Accessed: September 16, 2016,
https://www.doleta.gov/oa/bul04/Bul2004-10-att4.pdf

NNAAP 2014 Job Analysis Report for Nurse Aides. Accessed: September 16, 2016, https://www.ncsbn.org/15_2014NNAAP_Job_Analysis_vol65.pdf

Chapter 7

Is There a Demand for Male CNAs?

Do men become CNAs? Is there a demand for male CNAs?

We constantly hear these questions, so we decided this topic deserved its own chapter. Before we begin, we want to introduce you to Samuel. At the time we met him, Samuel was an aspiring CNA. (We only changed his name.)

Meet Samuel

We met Samuel while he was completing his clinical skills practicum at a small physician practice. Samuel is a native of Ethiopia. His country suffers from a shortage of medical personnel and limited access to healthcare, especially in the rural areas. He believes that becoming a CNA is an expedient path to a career in healthcare and a cost-effective one. One day he wants to return home to work as a healthcare provider. "I just want to help."

In the field on nursing, only one of every ten nurses is male. Surprisingly, the number of male nurses has tripled since the 1970s, according to the U.S. Census Bureau. Data for CNAs are lacking, but our colleagues in the field report a slight upward tick in the number of males entering the profession. Still, men are grossly underrepresented. Male CNAs are equally as capable and compassionate as females. So to put it simply, why aren't there more male CNAs? The obvious reason is that these jobs are considered caregiving occupations, and they are deep-rooted in the stereotypic notion that caregiving responsibilities should fall naturally to females.

Surprisingly, scientific data on how well males do as CNAs are extremely limited. So, we turned to non-conventional online content such as blogs, community groups and brief articles for possible explanations and insight. To mediate some of the bias typically found on the web, we searched for themes across a variety of sources and sites. Here's what we found:

1. Is there a demand for male CNAs? The answer appears to be "sort of." The demand for more healthcare workers in general, and specifically in nursing, has led to schools and facilities taking the next obvious step: recruiting male candidates. One can say the same for CNAs. So the uptake in male recruitment does not appear to be the result of an increase in male residents living in LTCFs, or of any gender-specific demands they might have .

2. The work culture of a facility may have an impact on how male CNAs are perceived. For example, they may be given different responsibilities simply because they are deemed physically stronger than females. They may be called upon more often to assist in lifting and turning, or they may be assigned to work with residents who are aggressive, combative, or are behaving inappropriately toward female staff. Also, it appears that in a few small facilities, males have been hired to provide care specifically to male residents, leaving female CNAs to attend to the larger majority female resident population.

3. Male CNAs may have a host of other gender-related stigmas to overcome. Male CNAs often are mistaken as physicians, physicians-in-training, and physician assistants. Also, in older generations and in many cultures, males are viewed as the authority figure, so the residents tend to defer to men. Consequently, in some facilities, males may be treated differently, sometimes even by staff. Because they are so few in number, male CNAs can be quite popular among the residents and staff. From our perspective, they certainly will stand out if they are good at what they do. However, if their performance is lagging, then everyone will know, too.

4. A resident's modesty could hinder a male CNAs' ability to administer care. Modest residents may simply feel more comfortable being cared for by a CNA of his or her own gender. Also, there is a growing number of culturally diverse residents living in nursing homes with strongly held beliefs that prohibit cross-gender touching of private areas. It is also interesting to note that sometimes it is not the resident voicing a complaint, but rather a

family member, expressing the concern over the gender of the caregiver.

As you learned about our friend, Samuel, becoming a CNA can be a calling, a passion to help others, and an entry into the field of healthcare. Gender does not, and should not, make a difference.

Now that you have a good understanding about CNAs, it is time to begin thinking about CNA training. The next several chapters will acquaint you with the basic requirements, what you need to consider when selecting a training program, and ways you can pay for it.

Chapter 8

BEFORE THE TRAINING — MEETING BASIC REQUIREMENTS

In this chapter, you will be able to determine if you meet the minimum requirements to enroll in a CNA training program. These criteria are common across the states, but still, it is wise to check with the agency in your state to see if there are changes or additional requirements beyond what we list here.

AGE

For the majority of states, you must be at least 18 years old to apply for a CNA certification. In a few states, like Alabama, Arizona, and Nebraska, the age limit is 16.

Education

At least a high school diploma or GED is required, but for states that allow for certification under the age of 18, the minimum education requirement is the eighth grade.

Competencies

Basic Skills (Placement Test). Most states require that you take and pass a **reading comprehension** test before you can enroll in CNA training. You might also get tested on your basic understanding of arithmetic. If you are going to be trained at a vocational or technical school or community college, you can take these tests at the school's assessment center.

Language. Most training schools require that you speak and understand English at a functional level. However, if English is not your first language, there are bilingual (English-Spanish) programs available (for example, W.F. Kaynor High School in Waterbury, CT, and Milwaukee Area Technical College).

Computer Literacy. Students must have basic knowledge of how to use a computer.

Pre-requisite Training

Some states require students to obtain a CPR certification before enrolling in a training program.

HEALTH AND DRUG SCREENING

You must be screened for drug abuse and for any signs of a medical or mental health condition to determine if it will hinder your ability to perform your job or put residents at risk. Also, you will be required to obtain and submit results of a TB skin test or chest x-ray before you can participate in the skills portion of the training. Some schools may require proof of immunization. If you plan to get your training in the winter, you may be required to get a flu shot.

BACKGROUND CHECK

Most states will perform a background check to screen for criminal convictions. Typically it consists of a fingerprint background check and criminal history records check. Not all states require a background check as a condition of training (e.g., South Carolina), but it may be a condition of your employment. If you have a criminal record (or live in a state that allows juvenile records to be unsealed) it will be prudent to learn what offenses would affect your employability as a CNA before you commit to a training program.

QUICK FACTS

A *reading comprehension* test is used to determine how well you understand what you read. It is typically a multiple choice test and is either administered manually (paper-and-pencil) or on a computer.

51

Chapter **9**

How to Select a Training Program

This chapter addresses how to find a CNA training program, what to look for, and the questions you should ask before you decide on selecting one.

The Landscape of Training Schools

According to a government report that identified 12,500 state-approved *CNA training* programs in the U.S., more than half (60 percent) are conducted by nursing homes. The remaining 40 percent are held at:

- Community colleges
- Vocational, technical and trade schools
- Non-profit organizations (e.g., American Red Cross, Goodwill Industries)

- Local Job Corps
- Local high schools
- Private for-profit schools
- U.S. Department of Veterans Affairs-designated training sites

WHERE TO FIND INFORMATION — RESPONSIBLE AGENCIES

If you do not know where to start, reach out to your state department of health (or public health) or the state *Board of Nursing (BON)* to get a list of approved schools. In the majority of cases, you can find information or links on their respective websites.

In some states, CNA training is regulated by other state offices or agencies. If your state appears below, start with that office.

State	Responsible Agency
AK	Commerce and Economic Development
AR	Office of Long Term Care
DE	Division of Long Term Care Residents Protection
FL, ME	Department of Education
GA	Medical Foundation
HI	Commerce and Consumer Affairs
KS, TX	Aging and Disability Services
IA	Inspections and Appeals
MO	Health and Senior Services
UT	Health Technology Certification Center
WV	Health & Human Resources Office of Health Facility

It is interesting to know that most states delegate the examination and the management of the state registry to a national testing company that administers the competency examinations. You can often find a list of the training schools, along with information about the competency exam requirements by state, on their websites. (We will present more information in Chapter 12.)

TRAINING SCHEDULES

CNA programs are quite flexible when it comes to training schedules. If you have personal, family, or work obligations, most likely you can find a training program that will accommodate your schedule. Classes are held during the day or evening, once or several times a week, weekdays, and on weekends. Training can be as brief as two weeks and as long as nine months. A typical training period lasts 6–12 weeks.

ONLINE TRAINING

Many online CNA training programs have emerged in recent years. While you may be able to complete the instruction component online, you still need to complete the required "hands-on," or clinical skills, portion of the training to be eligible for the CNA exam.

An example of a CNA training program with an online instruction component is Western Technical College in Wisconsin. It's "blended option" consists of 30 video hours of lecture, followed by live interaction with instructors and classmates for lab and clinical training.

ACCREDITATION AND STATE-APPROVAL

Throughout this book, we stress the importance of enrolling in a CNA training program that is state-approved. Sometimes aspiring students are confused when training schools cite a list of accreditations, but do not mention whether they are state-approved. Given the landscape of training venues, the confusion is understandable.

If you ever have applied for or attended college, you probably have heard something about accreditation. Higher education institutions that confer bachelor's and master's degrees — and specialty disciplines such as law, psychology, and nursing — voluntarily go through a rigorous process to become accredited. It is a testament of quality that is highly regarded and nationally recognized.

There are numerous accrediting agencies at the regional and national level. Examples of national accrediting bodies for *nursing practice* (i.e., registered and licensed practical nurses) are the Accreditation Commission for Education in Nursing (ACEN), the Commission on Collegiate Nursing Education (CCNE), and the National Council of State Boards of Nursing (NCSBN).

Currently, there is no *national* accreditation equivalent for CNAs. However, some state Boards of Nursing, empowered to act as the accrediting body for LPN and RN nursing programs, also *accredit* the CNA training programs in the state.

At the end of the day, make sure the organization that awarded the accreditation is recognized by your state. If there is no mention that the training program is state-approved, it is always a good idea to just check with the responsible state agency or BON. They will tell you if the accreditation is relevant to the state's approval of the training program.

ASK QUESTIONS

Once you find a state-approved training program that interests you, reach out to the training administrator, recruiter, or adviser and ask questions. In that way, you will be able to anticipate and resolve any challenges. Here are some examples:

Training schedule. *How often are new training sessions offered? When do classes meet? How long does it take to complete the training?*

Select a training program that will fit your schedule, complements your learning style and will allow you to learn at your own pace. In other words, do not enroll in an accelerated (2- or 4-week) course if you have no prior healthcare experience, do not have reliable transportation, and do not have the time or resources to commit to studying. Also, do not consider an accelerated program if it is hard for you to learn large amounts of material at a rapid pace. If you do not have your own transportation and must rely on a friend or relative to take you to and from class, be certain that the friend or relative is willing to commit their time over the course of several weeks or months.

Tuition and other costs. *What does the tuition cover?*

Some training programs cover the cost of textbooks and certain equipment and supplies. However, students generally are responsible for all ancillary costs (more in Chapter 10).

Financial aid. *What kinds of financial assistance are available? Is there a deadline to apply for assistance?*

Consider all other options before taking out a student loan. Know the difference between a grant, scholarship, and a student loan (more in Chapter 10).

Attendance. *What happens if I am late or miss a class?*

Because you are required to complete a specific number of training hours, programs are strict about attendance. Be sure you read and understand the school's attendance policy.

Experience of teaching staff. *What is the background and experience of the instructors?*

Training must be performed by, or be under the general supervision of, a Registered Nurse (RN) who has at least two years of nursing experience, one in providing long-term care. Other healthcare specialists might be included in the curriculum to teach courses in their specialty.

"Hands-on" clinical skills training. *Where do students go for their clinical training? How many hours per day/week am I required to spend in clinical training?*

You may have to travel to a clinical setting away from the facility or institution where classes are held. Unless there are multiple locations to choose from, consider your transportation costs and other logistics. Also, be aware that the facility might have specific days and times when you should report for your clinical supervision. If you are thinking about getting your training from an online school, find out how the school will help you satisfy this requirement.

Training successes. *What is the success rate of students who complete the training, pass the exam, and find employment? How long does it take for a student to find a job as a CNA after they are certified?*

A good training program will keep statistics. See an example at Wisconsin's Western Technical College: http://www.westerntc.edu/Programs/Placement.aspx?PROGRAM_NBR=305431

Or use this shortened URL: http://bit.ly/2bPMdar

Reviews from former students. *What did you like (or didn't like) about the training?*

First-hand information from someone who has successfully completed training can be extremely valuable. Always make sure the information is from a trustworthy source and from someone who can be objective.

The main point is don't be apprehensive about asking questions. If a training representative is not willing to take the time to answer your questions or direct you to the appropriate resources, that training program might not be worth your time and investment.

QUICK FACTS

1. High schools that offer CNA training, such as those in Maryland and North Carolina, have the same training standards and learning requirements as other CNA training programs.

2. **Boards of Nursing (BONs)** are state governmental agencies responsible for the regulation of nursing practice.

RESOURCES FOR THIS CHAPTER

Links to State resources in the Appendix.

American Red Cross: http://www.redcross.org/take-a-class/cna/cna-training

Goodwill Industries: http://www.goodwillsc.org/job-training/certifications/nurse-aide

Chapter 10

How to Pay for CNA Training (Or Get It for Free)

Tuition for CNA training can vary from a few hundred dollars to $2,500 or more, depending on where you live and who is conducting the training.

Along with a textbook, you are required to have certain equipment and supplies, such as scrubs, a stethoscope, and a blood pressure cuff. As we mentioned in the last chapter, some training programs will provide you with a few basic items because they are included in the costs of tuition. However, there are other expenses to consider. Take a look at this example:

A Snapshot of Costs

- Tuition
- Registration Fee

- Textbook(s)
- State Examination Fee
- Uniform (Scrubs/Shoes)
- Equipment (e.g., blood pressure cuff; stethoscope)
- State Exam Fee (to retake exam)

Other Possible Fees:

- Background Check
- CPR Certification
- Physical/Screening
- Vaccinations/Labs
- Transportation Costs
- Watch (with a secondhand)
- Malpractice Insurance
- Clinical site fees (I.D badge, parking, transportation)

Each school will provide you with a list of what you will need during the course of your training as well as what you can expect to pay for them. Sometimes you can find this information on the school's webpage. Also, if you are a single parent, you might need to factor in additional costs like child care. Make sure you have a good estimate of what it is going to cost you, and have a well-thought-out plan and budget on how you are going to pay for it all.

Now let's look at the ways you can finance your training. You can use:

- Your own money
- Gifts or loans (from family)
- Grants and scholarships

- A stipend from your employer
- Credit cards
- Student loans (government or private)
- Special funding or reimbursement sponsored the government, military, or a private organization

Most of you will be looking for some type of financial assistance for your training. The good news is that funding is available to either lower your overall costs or provide you with essentially free tuition, including reimbursement of your exam fees. The following sections cover a wide range of options and are worth exploring.

GRANTS AND SCHOLARSHIPS

Grants and scholarships are a stress-free way to pay for training because you don't have to pay back the money. Many people are familiar with these two types of funding but don't know how to access them. These funds are attainable through a variety sources — government; schools; corporations; non-profits; individual sponsors, as well as religious, professional, and social organizations.

The first type of funding you should look into is a grant or a *need-based* scholarship. Both are based solely on financial need. Grants are available from businesses, organizations, as well as the federal government.

The Goodwill Industries of Greater Michigan offers a need-based scholarship for CNA training. Many people are familiar with Goodwill as an organization to donate clothes and other goods to, but it also provides education and training for those who have difficulty finding jobs. At this particular Goodwill, one training scholarship is awarded to an aspiring CNA every training session. Check out the Goodwill Industries in your area to see if they offer a CNA training scholarship. You can view the requirements here:

http://www.goodwillgr.org/wp-content/uploads/2014/12/
Goodwill-CNA-Scholarship-Process.pdf

Or use this shortened URL: http://bit.ly/2bD2Hqc

Federally Funded Grants. A common, and relatively painless way to obtain financial assistance is from the federal government. If the training school qualifies for tuition payments through the federal student aid program, they will be eager to help you with the financial aid process. To get started, visit the U.S. Department of Education student aid website and apply for either a Federal Pell Grant or a Federal Supplemental Educational Opportunity Grant (FSEOG).

You will need to complete and submit the *Free Application for Federal Student Aid* (FAFSA). On the application you will identify the schools you are interested in attending for your training. You will get results, called an SAR (Student Aid Report), which will give you an Expected Family Contribution or EFC. Your EFC will be used to calculate your financial aid eligibility. Your SAR will arrive in about 3–5 days if you provide your email address. If you mail in your application, it may take up to two weeks to get your results. The schools you identified on your FAFSA will have access to your information electronically in just one day after it has been received and processed.

For more information, refer to this link:

https://studentaid.ed.gov/sa/fafsa

You can also apply for a federal student loan using the same FAFSA form. Remember, however, you must pay back a student loan, with interest. Your goal here is to explore and consider other options before taking out a student loan. A loan should be your last resort.

A special note about grants: While they do not have to be repaid, some grants may have stipulations requiring you to pay back all or part the money you received if you drop out of a training program. Make sure you read and are aware of your responsibility in order to qualify for the grant.

LONG-TERM CARE FACILITIES (NURSING HOMES)

Many LTCFs offer tuition-free CNA training. One way to get free training is through a work agreement or employment contract with the facility. You agree to work for the LTCF for a specified period after you become certified. In turn, the facility will train you free of charge. As a bonus, the employer might allow you to work at the nursing home while you get trained. Under OBRA, you are allowed to work up to four months in an LTCF while you pursue your CNA training.

The other way is through reimbursement. If you paid for your training out-of-pocket and are subsequently hired to work in a nursing home, you may be able to get reimbursed for the costs of your training, including the fees you paid to take the exam.

This reimbursement eligibility is articulated under OBRA (Federal regulation 42 CFR 483.152, 158). However, many students are either unaware of this opportunity, do not take advantage of it, or simply miss the deadline to apply. You must comply with the time requirements to receive reimbursement. Keep good records (i.e., the dates of your training, training receipts or invoices) and be sure to ask your prospective employer about it. Remember, it's not automatic. Here are the rules; there are no exceptions.

- You must be employed at a nursing facility within 12 months after you have completed your training and have passed the competency exam.
- Your first day of work at a nursing facility must occur after you completed your training and examinations.
- You must have paid your tuition out-of-pocket (that is, your own money). You cannot use grant or student loan funds.

MILITARY AID SOCIETIES

Military aid societies offer education assistance to service men and women and their eligible family members. These relief societies, along with the Red Cross, have collaborative agreements that make training accessible as well as affordable, even if you don't live near a military base. They are:

- Air Force Aid Society
- Army Emergency Relief
- Navy-Marine Corps Relief Society
- Coast Guard Mutual Assistance

With some research, you can locate specialized training grants or scholarships. For example, the Airman and Family Readiness Center (A&FRC) awards CNA training grants to the spouses of active duty military. Scholarships are not available at all bases, but the program has been steadily growing.

The Army Emergency Relief provides an extensive list of military and civilian education and scholarship resources. It is worth exploring to see if your CNA training will qualify. Here's the link:

http://www.aerhq.org/

State Employment and Training Programs

States typically set aside funds for job training to help people develop new skills and re-enter the workforce. Your state employment and training program may offer financial assistance for CNA training if you are unemployed, or receive some form of government income assistance.

Each state has an *Office of Adult and Continuing Education* or *Workforce and Continuing Education Department.* In some areas it is called the *One-Stop Career Center.* It is worth checking out. Let them know you are interested in CNA training, and they will help you locate financial aid resources, especially if you have little or no income or are a single parent. Refer to the link for the One-Stop Career Center:

http://www.careeronestop.org/LocalHelp/service-locator. aspx

Or use this shortened URL: http://bit.ly/2bycrAF

JOB CORPS

The Job Corps is a government program that provides education and technical training to low-income participants 16–24 years of age, or older if you have a documented disability. There is a Job Corps center in every state, and you also can also find them in high school vocational training departments. Reach out to your nearest Job Corps to see if there is a CNA training program in your area. The Job Corps also will assist you in getting a GED if you did not complete high school. You will be eligible to take the CNA exam after your training. The training program takes about eight to twelve months to complete.

THE WORKFORCE INVESTMENT ACT (WIA)

If you are unemployed and looking to start a new career as a CNA, explore training possibilities through a government-sponsored training program under the Workforce Investment Act (WIA). Training is free, and because they focus on training programs that take three months or less to complete, CNA training qualifies. You must meet eligibility requirements to participate in the program.

Also, there a program for adolescents and young adults between the ages of 14–21 under the Youth Workforce Investment Act. A participant must fall under one or more of the following criteria to be eligible:

- Have problems with basic literacy skills
- Did not complete high school

- Is homeless, a runaway or in foster care
- Is pregnant or a parent
- Is an offender
- Needs help completing an education program
- Needs help finding or holding onto employment (this includes youth with disabilities)

STATE BOARD OF NURSING, HEALTH OR PUBLIC HEALTH DEPARTMENT

As we discussed in Chapter 10, the Board of Nursing (BON), health or public health agency in your state should be able to help you locate a list of approved CNA training programs. From there you can contact individual schools directly about financial aid resources.

ONLINE TRAINING PROGRAMS

Online schools will help you identify student financial aid resources, such as grants and student loans that are either through the federal government or through commercial lending institutions, such as banks. Before considering an online program, make sure the training program is approved by your state. Also, consider other forms of student aid that you do not have to repay.

Lifetime Earning Credit
through Tax Deduction

If you or a family member (who claims you as a dependent on their taxes) is planning to pay out-of-pocket for your training (or it already has been paid), you might qualify for a Lifetime Learning Credit through the IRS.

There is no limit on the number of years you can claim the credit. It is worth up to $2,000 per tax return. Also, the training school must be a credible institution recognized by the U.S. Department of Education.

Use this interactive webpage to determine your eligibility for lifetime education credit

https://www.irs.gov/uac/Am-I-Eligible-to-Claim-an-Education-Credit%3F

Or use this shortened URL: http://bit.ly/2bpkHBi

There is also an app available to help you determine if you qualify for the deduction.

Now that you know how to fund your training, the next three chapters present an overview of the CNA training program, the competency exam, and tips on how to prepare.

Chapter 11

OVERVIEW OF THE CNA TRAINING PROGRAM

As we mentioned in previous chapters, state-approved CNA training programs must consist of at least 75 hours of instruction, which includes 16 hours of "hands-on" clinical skills training. The number of instructional hours varies across states. Some states go far beyond the minimum OBRA standards to address changes in nursing and safety practices. The results from a federal survey revealed nearly one-third of the states require a minimum of 100 hours or more of nurse aide training. Specifically, they are:

100 hours - Maryland, New Hampshire, New York, Rhode Island

105 hours - Indiana

120 hours - Arizona, District of Columbia, Florida, Idaho, Virginia

140 hours - Alaska

150 hours - California, Maine, Oregon

175 hours – Missouri

TRAINING CURRICULUM

The training curriculum consists of a broad range of subjects that includes:

1. **Basic Nursing Skills.** Taking and recording of vital signs; measuring and recording height and weight; caring for the resident's environment; recognizing and reporting abnormal changes in body functioning; caring for the dying resident.

2. **Personal Care Skills.** Bathing, grooming, dressing, and toileting; skin care; help with eating and hydration; transferring, positioning and turning.

3. **Mental Health and Social Service Skills.** How to respond appropriately to a resident's behavior; raising awareness of developmental issues related to the aging process; allowing the resident to make personal choices; accessing the resident's family as a source of emotional support.

4. **Cultural Competency.** Valuing diversity among residents; acquiring knowledge and skills necessary to work effectively across cultures to provide the best care possible.

5. **Caring for Cognitively Impaired Residents.** Addressing the behaviors of residents with *dementia*; commu-

nicating and responding to residents with cognitive impairments.

6. **Basic Restorative Skills.** Training the resident in self-care; using assistive devices in transferring, ambulation, eating and dressing; maintaining range of motion; proper turning and positioning in the bed and chair; bowel and bladder training; caring for and using prosthetic and orthotic devices.

7. **Residents' Rights.** How to provide privacy and maintain confidentiality; promoting residents' rights to make personal choices to accommodate their needs; giving assistance in resolving grievances and disputes; providing needed assistance in getting to and participating in resident and family groups and other activities; maintaining care and security of residents' personal possessions; promoting the resident's right to be free from abuse, mistreatment, neglect; and the need to report any instances of such treatment to appropriate nursing home staff; avoiding the need for restraints.

OBRA also requires at least 16 hours of training in the following areas prior to any direct contact with a resident:

1. Communication and interpersonal skills
2. Infection control
3. Safety and emergency procedures
4. Promoting resident independence
5. Respecting the rights of residents

Clinical Skills Training (Skills Portion)

Developing your clinical skills is the second component of your CNA training. You get "hands-on" experience by working in a real setting, such as a nursing home or hospital, and you get to apply what you've learned in the classroom. You will work under the supervision of a Registered Nurse and will have an opportunity to observe experienced CNAs.

The number of hours you need to complete your clinical training depends on the requirements of your state. In the same government survey cited earlier, more than half of the states require only 16 hours of supervised, hands-on training, which is the minimum required by OBRA. States with considerably higher minimum clinical hours are:

50-75 hours — Connecticut, Maine, New Hampshire, Oregon, Washington, West Virginia

80-95 hours – Alaska, California

100 hours — California, Missouri

Instructors

We mentioned earlier that the instructors in your CNA training program must be qualified. Training must be performed under the general supervision of a Registered Nurse (RN). The RN qualifications include a minimum of two years of nursing experience and at least one year of experience in long-term care. Other qualified specialists may serve as instructors.

In the next chapter, we present an overview of the competency examination.

Quick Facts

Dementia is a decline in mental ability that affects daily life due to aging or brain injury. It is characterized by memory loss, loss of reasoning abilities, and personality changes. Alzheimer's disease is a form of dementia.

Chapter 12

THE CNA EXAMINATION PROCESS

After completing a state-approved CNA training program, you must pass the competency examination. The purpose of taking the exam is to determine if you are sufficiently trained to work as an entry-level CNA in your state. Because state requirements vary, this chapter focuses on the main components of the examination process.

Most states participate in a competency examination process known as the *National Nurse Aide Assessment Program (NNAAP)*. Others collaborate with test service companies to develop state-specific assessments, or they use their own experts and resources to construct one.

Most states partner with a national organization such as the Red Cross or test service companies to function as test administrators. The three major test service companies are Pearson Vue, Prometric and Headmaster. Here is the breakdown:

Pearson Vue—Alabama, Alaska, California, Colorado, District of Columbia, Georgia, Louisiana, Maryland, Minnesota, Mississippi, New Hampshire, North Carolina, North Dakota, Pennsylvania, Rhode Island, South Carolina, Texas, Vermont, Virginia, Washington, Wisconsin, and Wyoming (also the Virgin Islands). Refer to Link:

www.pearsonvue.com/test-taker.asp

Prometric—Alabama, Arkansas, Connecticut, Delaware, Florida, Hawaii, Idaho, Michigan, Nevada, New Mexico, New York, and Oklahoma. Refer to Link:

http://www.prometric.com/en-us/Pages/home.aspx

Or use this shortened URL: http://bit.ly/2bD4J9M

Headmaster —Arizona, Montana, New Hampshire, Nevada, North Dakota, New Jersey (skills test), Ohio, Oklahoma, Oregon, South Dakota, Tennessee, and Utah. Refer to Link: http://hdmaster.com/

Red Cross—California, District of Columbia, Massachusetts, Maryland, New Hampshire, Pennsylvania, Vermont, Wisconsin, and Wyoming. Refer to Link:

http://www.redcross.org/ux/take-a-class

If your state has partnered with a test service company, you will find just about everything you need to prepare you for the examination on their website: application form, test schedules, locations of test centers, what to bring and what to wear. Requirements are specific to each state, so be sure to download the Candidate's Handbook for your state.

EXAM COMPONENTS

The competency exam consists of two components: a written and a clinical skills (performance) test.

Written test. The written portion consists of 40–70 multiple choice items, depending on your state regulations. Approximate time given to complete the test is about two hours, and this could also vary by state. At least 10 of these questions assess reading comprehension. The NNAAP and Prometric offer an oral or Spanish version of the test if English is not your second language, but you must request it when you submit your application to take the exam.

Clinical Skills Test. During the skills test, a proctor, usually an RN, will observe you carefully as you go through a care regimen with a live actor (or a mannequin) portraying the resident or patient. The test will take approximately 20–45 minutes, depending on your state's requirements. You must competently demonstrate at least five skills routinely used by CNAs in the following categories:

Personal Care: Bathing and personal grooming.

Use of Restorative Devices: Using and helping others use mobility aids, such as walkers and crutches, and devices that generally improve a patient's functions or lifestyle, such as catheters.

Mental Health Needs: Appropriately addressing a patient's mental health needs by interacting with patients who have a specific mental health diagnosis or psychosocial disability.

General Nursing Skills: Maintaining a clean environment, washing hands (yours and the resident's/patient's), recognizing symptoms and abnormalities.

Your score is based on how well you perform the tasks without being prompted (overall knowledge), the ability to follow procedures, your overall demeanor, and how well you communicate with the resident or patient while you are administering care.

COSTS

You will be charged a fee to take the exam. Some states charge a single fee while others charge separate fees for each portion (written and skills tests). Fees can range from $10 to $200. Most states require students who fail either the written or skills portion of the state exam to pay additional fees each time the test, or portion of the test, is retaken.

WHAT TO BRING

Detailed information is available in the Candidate's Handbook that you can download from the test service company. To give you a head's-up, you will need to bring valid identification, usually two forms of ID (for example, a government-issued picture ID; school ID, employment ID, or Social Security card). Make sure the name on your ID matches the information you provided on your application to take the test and make sure your ID has not expired. Check your handbook or the test administrator's website to find out which forms of ID are acceptable.

If you are taking a paper-and-pencil test, you will be required to bring pencils and an eraser. At some test centers, you will take a computerized test. If the center administers an on-line exam, you may be given the option of taking either the paper-and-pencil or the computerized version. Be aware that this option is not available at all test centers.

Some centers require that you bring along a watch with a second hand (e.g., Pennsylvania), or a partner or actor to play the role of the resident or patient (e.g., Massachusetts) for clinical skills portion. At some test facilities, you may also be asked to play the role of the patient or resident for another test taker.

WHERE TO GO

Typically, the exam is offered at multiple test center locations throughout the state. You may have the option of taking the exam at the site closest to you or another location if you need to take the test on a day that is more convenient for you. In some states, the training facilities double as approved testing sites, like the ones in Missouri.

TEST SCORES

States set their own passing scores. Some use a pass/fail system for one or both sections. Except for a few states that do not make their passing score public (Georgia, for example), you will know the passing score for each section of the test. Depending on the test administrator, you will be informed immediately after you have taken the test by way of a score report, or you may be notified at a later date.

In the next chapter, we present tips on how to prepare for your exam.

QUICK FACTS

The ***National Nurse Aide Assessment Program (NNAAP)*** is an examination program developed by the National Council of State Boards of Nursing. The NNAAP determines the minimal-level knowledge, skills, and abilities needed to become a CNA.

Chapter 13

TIPS ON HOW TO PREPARE FOR THE EXAM

Candidate handbooks offer valuable recommendations on how to prepare for the CNA exam. Some will even provide you with a separate study guide. Take the time to review these materials and take them seriously. If you need additional help, consider some of the practical tips we present in this chapter. They are suitable for just about any type of exam.

Establish a Study Schedule. Do not wait two weeks before the exam to start studying. Once your classes are over, continue a regular study schedule to review terms, concepts, take practice tests and review clinical skills until it's time to take the exam. Cramming is ineffective, especially for clinical skill exams. If you are a single parent and find it hard to carve out time to study, find someone to sit with your child for an hour or two. Or, if your children are old enough, try studying alongside them. If they are not thrilled with studying next to mom or dad, designate a specific time of the day or evening as "study time" in the home.

Participate in a Study Group. A small study group can be an effective way to see how well you know the material. Quizzing others (or being quizzed) can improve your understanding of concepts and help you remember information. Consider joining a small group (or starting one) with a good balance of average and above-average students so you can learn from each other, instead of one member serving as a "teacher" for the entire group. Also, make sure you chose members who want to study and are not looking to socialize or gossip. If a study group is not feasible, consider a study partner.

Practice Clinical Skills. Most students will tell you that they tend to be more anxious about this portion of the exam. The fact that the clinical skills portion has a higher failure rate than the written exam increases the anxiety level. Remember that simple memorization will not help you pass this component. You must practice! Some students find it helpful to talk through each step as they are performing it to perfect their skills.

Solicit Help from Family and Friends. Don't be afraid to ask for help. You've spent a lot of time, money and effort to reach this point, so be proud of your accomplishment. Ask them to assist you with test questions or let them play the role of the "resident" or "patient" so you can hone your skills.

Use Practice Tests and Flash Cards. Learning aids, such as practice tests and flash cards, can help to sharpen your understanding of terminology, concepts, and procedures. They are available in hard copy and online, for free and for purchase.

Practice tests will familiarize you with questions similar to the actual examination. If you are interested in viewing a sample of test questions developed by the NNAAP, here is the link:

https://www.asisvcs.com/publications/pdf/069912.pdf

Or use this shortened URL: http://bit.ly/2c9mysX

The free tests online generally consist of a small sample of test questions, while the paid tests contain full-sized sample versions of one or more tests. An answer key is also provided for each practice test. Some fee-based practice tests offer additional perks like electronic scoring. For a paying customer, Prometric will allow access to practice tests that are tied to the same internet test-based system you will use on the day of your test.

Apps. Practice tests and flash cards are also available through an app from Google PlayStore or Apple iTunes. Some are free, but the paid versions offer more user options. For example, you can customize the number of questions you want to answer as well as set a time limit to take the test.

Quizlet.com is an online education site that offers several shared study tools to help you master terms and concepts for the exam through quizzes, flash cards, and games. It can be used on your computer or laptop, or you can download their app. You can visit the site at http://www.quizlet.com. To view questions, type in "CNA test questions" and your state in the search tool.

When using practice tests, you eventually will need to take the full version under actual test conditions. Answer the same number of questions that will be on the actual exam and use the same time limit that you will be given to take the test. Select a place with no distractions. Turn off your cell phone, music and the TV.

An ideal place to take a practice exam is your local library. If your home is your only option, take the exam in a quiet room and during a period when you are likely to have a block of "quiet" time, for example, when family or roommates have gone to bed. If you have children, ask a friend or relative to watch over them for a couple of hours so you can take an exam.

Take Advantage of "Refreshers" When Available. Some training programs offer one-day "refresher" courses in preparation for the exam. The Red Cross, for example, offers an "Exam Cram" day when prospective test-takers can review content and practice their skills one or two days before the exam. This is a free session for their students. Other training schools may charge fees for their one- or two-day refreshers.

Arrive Early for the Exam. You will not be allowed to take the exam if you show up after the test has begun, so be sure to arrive early. Make sure you are familiar with the exam location. If possible, a few days before the exam, drive to the test center location to determine how much time you will need to get there during rush hour and where you can park.

The Night Before/Morning of the Exam. The evening before the exam, don't stay up late, party with friends, or drink alcohol. Double-check your list to ensure you have proper ID and any other required paperwork to gain entry into the test center. Do a light review of study materials and go to bed at a reasonable time. Make sure your phone has full power, especially if you rely on it for an alarm and GPS directions, and have a backup battery or battery charger handy. Set your alarm and have a backup if you are a hard sleeper or have a tendency to overuse the snooze button. The morning of the exam, eat a small breakfast. If you don't eat breakfast, consider a light snack so you don't get hunger pangs during the test.

Be Calm and Be Confident. Don't panic! It's okay to feel a little anxious, but excessive worrying will hurt your performance. These tests are not designed to trick you or prevent you from becoming certified. Executing a well-thought-out study plan in advance of your exam will give you the confidence you need to pass.

Chapter 14 describes the next step after you have passed the competency examination—placement in the state CNA registry.

Chapter 14

THE CNA STATE REGISTRY

Under OBRA, each state must establish and maintain a registry of Certified Nursing Assistants. After you pass the exam and apply for your certification, you will be included in your state's CNA registry. The registry identifies individuals who have completed training and are found to be competent to work in long-term care facilities. The registry is maintained either by the state or a test service company such as Pearson Vue.

A state's registry contains the individual's: 1) name; 2) identifying information; 3) date eligible for placement in the registry, and 4) any substantiated finding of abuse, neglect, or theft. Thus, another objective of state CNA registries is to ensure that LTCFs do not employ individuals with **substantiated findings.** States are required to update the registry records with a substantiated finding within 10 working days of the ruling.

CNAs who have not performed any work or work-related services for 24 consecutive months typically are removed from the registry unless the records include a substantiated finding. However, according to a government survey, removal due to inactivity it is not a certainty. You also should be aware that records with substantiated findings are never removed from the registry.

Most states periodically verify the names of CNAs on the registry's active list. While some states require the facility to do the verifying, you may have to prove that you are still active as a CNA. Be proactive and keep copies of all your documents because records — even electronic ones — can get lost, contain errors or get deleted, or a facility where you once worked may no longer be in operation. Allowable evidence is a letter from the employer, a pay stub showing that you have worked at least eight hours at a facility during the past 24 months, or a *W-2* (or 1099) earnings statement from your employer.

The next chapter provides some tips to put you on the fast track to finding employment.

QUICK FACTS

1. *Substantiated findings* are investigative findings that support (i.e., prove) reported allegations of inappropriate conduct by a healthcare professional toward a resident or patient. Examples include abuse, neglect, and theft.

2. A *W-2,* (or a 1099 if you are a contractor) is a form that your employer sends to the IRS at the end of the tax year. The W-2 shows how much you earned and how much has been withheld for taxes. (If you are issued a 1099, it will show how much you earned.) Usually, you will get a copy of the W-2 or 1099 in January of the following year that you worked.

RESOURCES IN THIS CHAPTER

State Nurse Registries Address and Phone numbers

https://www2.ncdhhs.gov/dhsr/hcpr/links.html

Chapter 15

TIPS TO HELP YOU LAND YOUR FIRST CNA JOB

Some CNAs say it can be difficult landing that first job. It is frustrating to be told you need experience, but you can't gain experience without first getting a job. It's a classic career Catch-22 for many who are entering the workforce for the first time, starting a new career, or have limited work experience.

Most often, a CNA's first job is in a nursing home. Some entered into an agreement with the nursing home to work for a specified period in return for their training. If you did not negotiate an agreement ahead of time and find yourself newly certified but unemployed, don't get discouraged. While it may be a challenge, your persistence will pay off. We all have been there, and eventually, we get hired.

Consider these tips:

1. **Take advantage of resources while in training.**
    Take full advantage of the resources around you. Some
    training programs have career or job placement cen-
    ters. Reach out to your career counselor at school, your
    training instructor, or the facility's Director of Nursing
    (DON). Talk to fellow classmates and see what avenues
    they are exploring.

2. **Be open to work in any setting.** Many new CNAs flock
    to the hospitals hoping to land their first job. The prob-
    lem is that hospitals receive a high number of appli-
    cations. They can afford to be more selective and will
    choose candidates with more training and experience.
    Consider other workplaces where CNAs are in high de-
    mand, like nursing homes, and don't forget temporary
    or contract positions. Do not think of this option as
    "settling." You are putting your knowledge and skills to
    good use and gaining experience that eventually can
    lead you to the work setting of your choice.

3. **Keep in touch with former classmates.** Your old class-
    mates can be good resources because many of them also
    will be looking for work. "Friend" them on social media,
    text, or email them for an update. You may learn that
    the facility that hired them might have other positions
    to fill.

4. **Go online.** Check out websites that advertise job vacan-
    cies and sign up for alerts if available. Examples are:

    ● Employment Websites (e.g., Indeed, Simply Hired,
      Monster, CareerBuilder)

- Federal Government Websites (e.g., USAJobs as well as specific government agencies, such as the Department of Veteran Affairs)

- State and County Government Websites

- Social Media Sites (Facebook, Twitter, Instagram, LinkedIn)

- Career-oriented Websites (e.g., Nurse.com, NurseRecruiter.com)

- Professional Associations (e.g., National Association of Health Care Assistants; National Network of Career Nursing Assistants)

A word of caution about using a public computer. If you use a public computer to complete and submit your application (e.g., at a library or a virtual office location like FedEx Office), take a flash drive with you to save an application or to upload your resume. Do not save information on any public computer. Also, remember to log off your job account page and close the browser so that no one else can come after you and access the page with your personal information.

5. **Attend job fairs.** Employers with positions to fill will send their representatives to job fairs to meet with and interview job seekers. Some employers are looking to fill jobs quickly. Prospective workers can learn about the company as well as ask questions about the job and about company benefits. Also, many job seekers find it advantageous to reach out to a real person who is likely to remember them, rather than applying to companies "anonymously" online.

6. **Volunteer.** Sign up to be a volunteer at a nursing facility, if only for a few hours a week. You will not be able

to perform your official CNA duties, but you can assist staff in the activities department, playing games with the residents and escorting them on outings and day trips. Your volunteerism will demonstrate your passion and commitment. When a position becomes available, your familiarity with the facility and the residents could give you an advantage, and you can add the experience to your resume.

7. **Talk to friends and family members**. Be proud of your accomplishment and let your friends and family know you can use their help in finding a job. In essence, you are expanding your personal network through theirs. There might be someone in their social or professional network who could help you land that first job as a CNA.

8. **Contact agencies directly**. Contact LTCFs, hospitals, and other healthcare facilities in your local area and inquire about job openings. You can search the internet using keywords such as "long-term care facilities" or "nursing homes" to find facilities in your area, or you can peruse the local telephone directory available at the library. It is better that you avoid emailing or texting. Instead, call the agency and ask to speak with someone in the human resources department who can give you information about CNA vacancies and how to apply.

9. **Be proactive in your job search.** Many newly-licensed CNAs are quickly discouraged when the employer advertises for an experienced CNA. The vast majority of employers do. However, *carefully* read the job vacancy announcement. If it says experience is "preferred but not required," apply for the job and see what happens.

10. **Show your "potential" with a prospective employer.**
During the interview, a prospective employer will try to determine if there's any benefit to hiring you. While you don't have the experience, you can give the employer other reasons to hire you by demonstrating that you have the potential to be successful on the job. Show that you have a positive attitude, good communications skills, enthusiasm, and a basic knowledge of the organization. In other words, know enough about the facility to be able to answer questions about why you want to work there. You can find information about the facility or the company from their website.

After you have landed your first job as a CNA, Chapters 16 and 17 offer information and insights that will help you further develop your career in healthcare and avoid common mistakes on the job.

Chapter 16

Keeping Your Job and Growing Professionally

Once you are placed on the state's registry, you are on your way to establishing your career as a CNA. Your first year on the job will be both exciting and challenging. You are fulfilling your dream and should be very proud of your accomplishment.

However, being in a new work setting, learning new names and faces, and getting up to speed on administrative policies and procedures can be a little nerve-wracking at first. There are many online tips to help you get beyond those initial jitters. In this chapter are a few suggestions that we hope will help kick-start your career by 1) avoiding some of the more common stumbling blocks when you are starting out; 2) maintaining your certification; and 3) developing your career.

MAINTAINING PROFESSIONAL STANDARDS

1. As a CNA, it is important to know how to conduct your-self at work. What you say and do will have an impact on how other CNAs are perceived, the credibility of the facility, and the company as a whole. Maintain a professional demeanor with the resident's family and friends, members of your team, and other facility staff.

2. Once you are hired, you will go through an employee orientation. You will get an overview of the company's policies and procedures. Most likely you will be given an employee handbook or you could download one through your employee online account. The biggest mistake of novice workers is to ignore it and become completely dependent on co-workers to provide this information. Always read the handbook for yourself, refer to it as needed, and ask the appropriate staff to clarify policies that you are unsure about.

3. Stay within your scope of duties and responsibilities as a CNA. Perform your tasks as you were trained to perform them. Avoid cutting corners, even if you see a co-worker doing it. Your nurse supervisor should approve new procedures or modifications of current ones. Whenever you are unsure about performing a task, ask your nurse supervisor.

4. Maintain a good work record by adhering to your work schedule and reporting to work on time. If being late for work is unavoidable, or you are unable to report to work, contact your supervisor *as early as possible*. For example, if you know the evening before that you will

not make it to work, don't call 15 minutes before your shift begins.

5. Respect the rights, privacy, and personal belongings of residents (refer to Chapter 17 for further discussion).

6. Be tolerant and respectful of residents with other cultural belief systems and values, particularly as they pertain to health, illness, death, medical and family. Don't allow your cultural beliefs and other personal attitudes to influence how you interact and care for residents.

7. Maintain good personal hygiene. Avoid heavy perfume, cologne, or shaving lotion; oversized jewelry; long, odd-shaped or jewelry-studded fingernails; and heavy make-up.

8. View constructive feedback as an opportunity to improve your skills. Do not take it personally and get angry with your supervisor.

9. Whenever possible, volunteer to work overtime when the facility is understaffed.

10. Show interest in, and be willing to learn, new tasks and take on additional CNA responsibilities.

11. Stay abreast in your field and keep your skills current by attending the required in-service training and other staff development seminars.

CONTINUING EDUCATION

You must participate in a minimum of 12 hours of in-service training every year to maintain your certification. Nursing homes and other long-term care facilities participating in a

Medicaid or Medicare funding program must provide training on the following topics:

1. Fire prevention and response

2. Emergency procedures and preparedness

3. Resident's rights

4. Infection control and prevention

5. Proper use of restraints

6. Confidentiality of resident information

7. Care of the cognitively impaired

In conjunction with in-service training, CNAs must have their performance evaluated at least once every 12 months. Performance problems identified in employee evaluations often form the foundation for new training topics.

RENEWING YOUR CERTIFICATION

Remember to renew your certification. If nurse assistants must be certified to work at your facility, it is important that you renew on time.

Renewal typically is every two years. In many cases, you can renew online.

You will need to renew before the expiration date. Most states will send you a notice 30–60 days before expiration. This is one reason why maintaining an active physical address is mandatory for state registries. You also will have to pay a fee to renew.

To get your certification renewed, you must show continuous employment as a CNA for the minimum number of hours as required by your state. OBRA requires 12 hours annually. Also, you cannot have any substantiated complaints of abuse or neglect in the registry.

Expired Certification. If you missed the renewal deadline, most states allow a grace period, and you may only need to show proof of activity of your continuing education hours and a pay late fee and your renewal fee. Beyond that period, you will be required to retake the examination, and pay associated fees all over again (like a background check).

RECIPROCITY

If you are looking to move to another state to be closer to extended family, for a job opportunity, or simply for a fresh start in a new environment, you may qualify to work as a CNA in your new state without going through the retraining and certification process. The process is known as applying for *reciprocity*. You must have met the competency evaluation requirements of OBRA, have an active certification, and be in good standing in the state that you are leaving. You can start by contacting that state's Registry, the Board of Nursing (BON), or the responsible agency to find out what forms you will need to submit to your new state. You can get the number for an out-of-state BON by going to the National Council State Board of Nursing (NCSBN) website here: https://www.ncsbn.org/725.htm

Again, be sure to keep good records of your employment history (including continuing education hours, certificates, etc.) should you need them.

Using Military Experience to Apply for Reciprocity. Using your military medical experience to qualify as a civilian CNA will depend greatly on the state. In Washington, for example, you may be eligible for reciprocity based solely on your military experience. Other states, like North Carolina, require that you submit a *training waiver* request and take the state's competency exam. Then there are other states, such as Nebraska, that do not recognize military experience and require both CNA training from a state-approved school and passing of the competency exam.

CAREER ADVANCEMENT

Although the training you receive as a CNA is at the entry-level, you can acquire credentials that will allow you to specialize or grow professionally. As we mentioned in Chapter 3, some states allow for advancement within the CNA job category (for example, Advanced Certified Nursing Assistant or Certified Nurse Assistant II).

Pursuing a higher credential involves a combination of additional training, assessment, experience, and in some instances, an endorsement or recommendation from a supervisor (e.g., Virginia).

There are also other areas of specialization, such as:

- Wound Care Assistant

- Patient Care Technician/Assistant
- Home Health Care Assistant/Aide (considered a specialty within a CNA training program in some states)

Organizations such as the National Council of State Boards of Nursing (NCSBN) or the American Board of Wound Management can provide information about CNA credentials.

GOING FURTHER

You can use your certification and experience to pursue other career objectives in healthcare. We will cover just a few here.

You can continue your education by pursuing degrees in nursing, such as a Licensed Practical Nurse (LPN) or Registered Nurse (RN). CNA-to-RN bridge programs are available, which shortens the education/training time.

With continued education and training, you can also transition into areas such as food service, environmental (infection) control, laboratory services, and diagnostic (radiology) services. There is also the administrative side of healthcare, such as research, quality assurance, and human resources.

Your Director of Nursing (DON) can be a helpful resource when you are ready to take that step.

QUICK FACTS

Reciprocity—a process by which a CNA from one state qualifies for certification in another state.

Chapter 17

CURRENT AND TRENDING ISSUES FOR CNAS

In previous chapters, we discussed the necessary steps you should take to start building your career as a CNA. In addition to keeping abreast of practices and procedures, new tools and technologies, and maintaining an active certification, you should also stay abreast of the issues, challenges, and controversies in your field. This chapter discusses both current and trending issues.

EMPLOYMENT OUTLOOK

Because of the high demand, the job outlook for CNAs is excellent. Employment is projected to grow by 18 percent from 2014 to 2024. According to the U.S. Bureau of Labor Statistics (BLS), the rate is *faster than the average* for all other occupations. This projection does not include facilities having to refill positions due to high turnover.

CNA Pay and Benefits

The BLS 2016–17 Occupational Outlook Handbook lists the *median* annual salary for CNAs at $25,090. This equates to about $12/hour during a regularly scheduled work week. After taxes and other deductions, new CNAs may be disappointed with their earnings, but there is good news: with overtime, the hourly rate increases to approximately $18/hour.

Furthermore, there is a nationwide momentum to increase the minimum hourly wage in the U.S. to $15/hour. While this has yet to become a national law, a handful of states and cities have already implemented the new minimum wage and several others will phase it in over the next few years.

Your geographic location, as well as your level of experience, can affect your pay and benefits. Larger metropolitan areas tend to pay more than smaller cities and towns; however, the cost of living in larger cities is higher and should be taken into account.

High Turnover, Poor Retention

Despite the more than 2.8 million names reported in CNA state registries across the country, nearly half of those are inactive. There is significant turnover among CNAs, especially in long-term care, resulting in a continual staffing shortage.

Turnover is affected by a variety of factors. The main reasons cited are low pay and benefits, few opportunities for advancement and low job satisfaction. It is noteworthy that some CNAs move on to further their career in healthcare as LPNs or RNs, in administration or in other health-related fields. Most importantly, some CNAs remain in the field for years, and others long enough to retire.

INJURIES

A CNA's job can be physically demanding, and that increases your risk of injury. According to the BLS, workers in nursing and residential care facilities have the highest injury rates of any occupational setting, higher than construction workers and truck drivers. Injuries can stem from a variety of causes, including lifting residents, behaviors by aggressive residents (e.g., bites), and accidents from misusing equipment. Facilities have stepped up their in-service training to try to reduce employee injuries.

RESIDENTS AND MENTAL HEALTH

Increasingly, individuals are entering nursing homes with serious behavioral and mental health issues, leaving some nursing home administrators, and DONs strained. Few nursing homes employ appropriate mental health professionals — such as licensed clinical psychologists — to provide appropriate interventions. The primary reason is the reimbursement limits placed by Medicare for behavioral health services performed by psychologists.

That leaves you, as the front-line attendant, to interact with and respond to residents with serious emotional and mental challenges on a daily basis. Some residents might display anger and aggressive behavior due to dementia or other psychiatric issues. Others might suffer from **hallucinations** or **delusions** or are clinically depressed. Remember always to reach out to your nurse supervisor if you need help, and seek additional training.

WORK-LIFE BALANCE

We all strive to maintain a balance between our work life and our personal life. However, it is not easily achieved. You may be asked to take another shift at the last minute because the facility is short-staffed, even though you have a PTA meeting to attend; or, you may have to report to work even though your child is sick. As a CNA, be prepared to juggle demanding schedules. It helps to have a good backup plan and support system in place.

RESIDENTS AND HIPAA

Many healthcare workers thought it would be easy protecting patient information under the **HIPAA** laws. However, in practice, there have been many challenges to that assumption. With information readily accessible, it isn't easy keeping information confidential. As we wrote in Chapter 1, CNAs spend more time with residents and patients than any other member of the healthcare team. You become increasingly at risk for mishandling confidential information whenever you form close relationships with residents, their families, caregivers, friends (including those that live in the facility), and other healthcare staff.

According to HIPAA, you cannot disclose a resident's personal health information (PHI). Any comment you make about the resident's health can result in serious repercussions if the caregiver, family, friend, or a co-worker does not have the right to that information. It makes no difference how trivial the information seems; it's not yours to give. However, it's not a problem for residents to share information with one another, which is common in LTCFs where bonds of friendship are formed.

GENERATIONAL AND CULTURAL DIVERSITY

Every generation and culture has beliefs, values, customs, interests, attitudes, and behaviors that are unique to them. Often these differences are overlooked, or even ignored, by professional caregivers.

Contemporary healthcare practices note the importance of acknowledging generational and cultural differences and understanding how they affect residents' views on health, medicine, and treatment. As a CNA, you are professionally bound to respect generational and cultural differences and not force your views on others. Focus instead on making the resident or patient the center of care (***patient-centered care***). Be proactive in learning about diversity and inclusion through in-service training and other courses, and make a concerted effort to learn the particular backgrounds of the residents you serve. You can learn a lot by simply asking them questions.

Residents' Rights and Social Media

These days, just about everyone seems to have a smart phone and at least one social media account. Some people spend a lot of time taking selfies and sometimes that includes everything around them, including unwilling participants. Too often, little consideration is given to the privacy of others. Capturing the activities of your day to keep friends and family entertained is one thing, but taking pictures at work could cost you your job.

Using your camera phone at work can lead to serious repercussions. Nursing home residents have specific rights under the law, and that includes their privacy. After all, it is their home. Posting photos without the resident's permission may violate HIPAA, which carries both civil and criminal penalties for violating confidentiality and privacy.

Unfortunately, a small percentage of CNAs have been found guilty of violating these rights. Recent news articles have described certain CNAs posting and sharing improper photos and videos of nursing home residents on social media. It is not only a public embarrassment to the resident, but also to his or her family and the facility. Furthermore, it can also trigger inspections, lawsuits, and possible criminal charges.

No matter how innocent you believe your photos are, you can avoid the possibility of violating a resident's rights by resisting the temptation to take and post pictures of your workplace to your Facebook, Instagram, Snapchat, or other social media account. Even if you have their permission, some residents may give consent to avoid possible conflict or retaliation. Also, if a resident's cognitive functioning is declining, he or she might be incapable of granting you permission. Keep in mind that once an image is uploaded, you have no control over where it goes, to whom, or how it is used. If your camera phone is not a required device to perform your job, don't use it. Instead, remain professional and focus on giving the best care you can provide.

QUICK FACTS

1. A *median* salary is similar to the mean salary or average salary, except there's an adjustment made for those making very high or very low salaries, called outliers. Outliers can distort the "true average" salary. By using a median, the midpoint (or middle) is determined among the group of salaries, ranged from low to high. It marks the salary where half of the CNAs will likely be paid more than the midpoint and the other half will be paid less than the midpoint.

2. A *hallucination* is seeing, hearing or smelling something that doesn't exist, except in the mind of the person experiencing the perception. A *delusion* is a preoccupation with a false belief that cannot be accounted for by the person's background or intelligence; e.g., a belief about being poisoned or followed.

3. *HIPAA* is the acronym for the *Health Insurance Portability and Accountability Act.* It pertains to a set of rules and regulations regarding the documentation and privacy of personal health information or (PHI).

4. *Patient-centered care*, according to the National Institute of Medicine, is "care that is respectful of, and responsive to, individual patient preferences, needs, and values, and ensuring that patient values guide all clinical decisions."

RESOURCES FOR THIS CHAPTER

Bureau of Labor Statistics, U.S. Department of Labor, Occupational Outlook Handbook, 2016–17 Edition, Nursing Assistants and orderlies.

http://www.bls.gov/ooh/healthcare/nursing-assistants.htm
Accessed: April 09, 2016.

Ornstein, Charles, ProPublica. Inappropriate Social Media Posts by Nursing Home Workers, Detailed (December 15, 2015). Accessed: February 2, 2016.

https://www.propublica.org/article/inappropriate-social-media-posts-by-nursing-home-workers-detailed

Chapter 18

GOING FORWARD

Congratulations! You stayed the course and demonstrated two important attributes that will help in your pursuit to become a CNA: commitment and discipline.

We hope that we answered the majority of your questions about becoming a CNA, and with this knowledge, you can decide whether it is the right career path for you. In closing, here are a few thoughts we would like to share with you.

As a CNA of the new millennium, you will be among a group of paraprofessionals who are changing people's perceptions about what it means to provide basic care.

For many of you, becoming a CNA will be an entry into the field of healthcare and you will advance to other areas. However, not everyone leaves their CNA credential behind. In just about every setting, there are CNAs who genuinely love what they do and would rather not do anything else.

If healthcare truly is your calling, you will find satisfaction in the simplest of ways. Among them, the heartfelt appreciation from the residents you care for, and a personal fulfillment knowing that you made their later years happier, safer and meaningful.

If you decide to become a CNA, you will have a credential that will always be in demand, no matter where you live, and the rewards, we feel, will be priceless.

We wish you the best of luck in your career endeavors!

About the Authors

Sheilah Mara

Sheilah Mara is a veteran researcher, educator, behavioral health consultant and technical writer. She lives in the Washington, D.C., area and has worked in mental health in a variety of managerial and training positions, offering a broad and unique perspective on clinical and programmatic issues affecting long-term care for seniors. She holds a doctoral degree in clinical-community psychology.

Dr. Mara presently writes on a wide range of topics in behavioral health and consults with psychology students and professionals on measurement and statistics, assessment and program evaluation, quality improvement, and organizational issues.

From a military background that includes her tenure as a Scientist in the U.S. Public Health Service Commissioned Corps, Dr. Mara is used to working in different environments, including nursing homes, community organizations, educational institutions, government programs, and private practice, all along the East Coast.

When she isn't working or writing, Sheilah relaxes with one of her many hobbies such as listening to music, reading Jane Austen books, or watching old black-and-white movies. She also enjoys cooking, trips to the beach, bargain-hunting with friends, and star gazing.

TERRY B. THOMAS

Terry B. Thomas is a retired licensed nursing home administrator, with more than 30 years of experience in healthcare administration, and has experience in managing both private and government-operated facilities in Washington, D.C. He holds a doctorate in Health Care Administration.

Dr. Thomas played a key role in the implementation of federal nursing home regulations and is also a writer, planner, and organizer, as well as an accomplished public speaker.

Dr. Thomas held senior executive positions in Washington, D.C., serving under two of the city's mayors and addressing many key healthcare issues in the city. He also served on the Board of Trustees at the University of the District of Columbia, where he chaired the academic committee that approved training and degree programs in nursing.

Since retiring, Terry has found more time to enjoy fishing, listening to his extensive collection of blues and jazz music, reading and watching televised Congressional hearings. He is also an avid viewer of political talk shows and follows news events on national healthcare with interest.

CONNECT WITH US!

Did You Like Our Book?
Reach out with Feedback!

Thank you for your purchase. If you enjoyed this book, please post an Amazon rating and a short review. Your support makes a difference. It takes less than a minute and we read all the reviews. We are firm believers in quality and with your feedback we can make future updates of this book even better.

Also, if you find any typos or errors, please let us know by sending an email to us at cnapublications@washbehavioral-health.com

PASS IT ON!

If you like our book, let your friends know by posting a comment on social media. In fact, why not send a selfie of you reading our book?! If you are a member of the Goodreads community, don't forget to share your comments there as well. You will help others who are seeking information, and of course, we will be grateful for your contribution.

Be the First to Learn When Our Next Book is Coming Out!

Stay connected to learn about our new upcoming titles in behavioral health and long-term care. Sign up at newbooks@washbehavioralhealth.com.

In addition, be on the lookout for periodic surveys on Facebook and Twitter where we will ask readers to help us decide on future book topics. Be sure to vote, because every vote counts!

Appendix

Links to CNA Resources by State, U.S. Territories and the District of Columbia

Here are helpful links to resources on Certified Nursing Assistants by state, U.S. territories and the District of Columbia so you will have the most up-to-date information available.

The majority of the links will direct you to a government agency website. Any problems or navigational issues we encountered are noted. Because websites are constantly being updated, the page may have moved or you may encounter a broken link. If you do, use the search tool on the website's homepage and type in "certified nurse assistant", "nurse aide" or "CNA" as keywords.

If your state contracts with a test administrator, you can also find information on their website. Links are available at the end of the state list.

Alabama

https://dph1.adph.state.al.us/NurseAideRegistry/(S(nchvn-ji3xle2fs45jpoohl45))/FAQ.aspx

Shortened URL: http://bit.ly/2bGXonz

See #9, Frequently Asked Questions. See also Pearson Vue, Prometric, and Headmaster.

ALASKA

https://www.commerce.alaska.gov/web/cbpl/ProfessionalLicensing/NurseAideRegistry.aspx

Or use shortened URL: http://bit.ly/2bhZiLp

See also Pearson Vue.

ARKANSAS

http://humanservices.arkansas.gov/dms/oltcDocuments/natp.pdf

Or use shortened URL: http://bit.ly/2bUNXhy

See also Prometric.

ARIZONA

https://www.azbn.gov/#

CALIFORNIA

https://www.cdph.ca.gov/CERTLIC/OCCUPATIONS/Pages/AidesAndTechs.aspx

Or use shortened URL: http://bit.ly/2eyayVp

See also Pearson Vue and Red Cross.

COLORADO

https://www.colorado.gov/pacific/dora/Nursing

See also Pearson Vue.

CONNECTICUT

http://www.ct.gov/dph/cwp/view.asp?a=3121&q=389390

Or use shortened URL: http://bit.ly/2cI1i2E

See also Prometric.

DELAWARE

http://www.dhss.delaware.gov/dltcrp/cnareg.html

See also Prometric.

DISTRICT OF COLUMBIA

http://cc.udc.edu/workforce_development/healthcare_career_pathway

Or use shortenedURL: http://bit.ly/2bUNN9U

See also Pearson Vue, Red Cross.

FLORIDA

http://floridasnursing.gov/licensing/certified-nursing-assistant-examination/

Or use shortened URL: http://bit.ly/2bhm60z

See also Prometric.

GEORGIA

https://www.mmis.georgia.gov/portal/PubAccess.Nurse%20Aide/tabId/74/Default.aspx

Or use shortened URL: http://bit.ly/2bD4efX

Scroll to Section III, Frequently Asked Questions. See also Prometric.

Hawaii

http://health.hawaii.gov/docd?s=cna&type=usa

http://cca.hawaii.gov/pvl/programs/nurse/

See also Prometric.

Idaho

http://healthandwelfare.idaho.gov/Medical/LicensingCertification/FacilityStandards/CertifiedNursingAssistants/tabid/282/Default.aspx

Or use shortened URL: http://bit.ly/2ewYxO6

See also Prometric.

Illinois

http://dph.illinois.gov/topics-services/health-care-regulation/health-care-worker-registry/cna-facts

Or use shortened URL: http://bit.ly/2bPRM8V

Indiana

http://www.state.in.us/isdh/20510.htm

Iowa

https://dia.iowa.gov/health-facilities/certified-nursing-assistants

Or use shortened URL: http://bit.ly/2bXBI87

Kansas

https://www.kdads.ks.gov/commissions/scc/health-occupations-credentialing\

Or use shortened URL: http://bit.ly/2bBFSPt

KENTUCKY

http://kbn.ky.gov/knar/Pages/faqknar.aspx

LOUISIANA

http://new.dhh.louisiana.gov/index.cfm/directory/detail/7440

Or use shortened URL: http://bit.ly/2eyaRzx

See also Pearson Vue.

MAINE

http://maine.gov/dhhs/dlrs/cna/faq/index.shtml

MARYLAND

http://mbon.maryland.gov/Pages/cna-index.aspx

MASSACHUSETTS

http://www.mass.gov/eohhs/gov/departments/dph/programs/hcq/nurse-aides/

Or use shortened URL: http://bit.ly/2bplORo

See Red Cross.

MICHIGAN

https://michigancenterfornursing.org/content/frequently-asked-questions

Or use shortened URL: http://bit.ly/2bD42O3

Click link under Question 1. See Prometric.

MINNESOTA
http://www.health.state.mn.us/divs/fpc/profinfo/narinfo/aboutnar.html

Or use shortened URL: http://bit.ly/2cSpY70

See Pearson Vue.

MISSISSIPPI
http://msdh.ms.gov/msdhsite/_static/30,0,83,74.html

See Pearson Vue.

MONTANA
https://dphhs.mt.gov/CNA

See Headmaster.

MISSOURI
http://health.mo.gov/safety/cnaregistry/cna.php

NEBRASKA
http://dhhs.ne.gov/publichealth/Pages/crlCNAHome.aspx

Or use shortened URL: http://bit.ly/2d9ZfAC

NEVADA
http://nevadanursingboard.org/licensure-and-certification/how-to-apply-for-certification/

Or use shortened URL: http://bit.ly/2bD3Z4y

See Prometric; Headmaster.

New Hampshire

https://www.nh.gov/nursing/nursing-assistant/index.htm

See also Pearson Vue; Red Cross; Headmaster.

New Jersey

http://www.nj.gov/health/healthfacilities/nacert.shtml

See Headmaster.

New Mexico

https://nmhealth.org/about/dhi/hflc/prop/nar/

Type "nurse aide" in search box and you will be redirected to Prometric

New York

https://labor.ny.gov/stats/olcny/certified-nurse-aide.shtm

See also Prometric.

North Carolina

https://www2.ncdhhs.gov/dhsr/hcpr/guide.html

See also Pearson Vue.

North Dakota

http://www.ndhealth.gov/hf/North_Dakota_certified_nurse_aide.htm

Or use shortened URL: http://bit.ly/2bBEyfe

See also Pearson Vue; Headmaster.

OHIO

https://www.odh.ohio.gov/odhprograms/dc/natrg/na1.aspx

Or use shortened URL: http://bit.ly/2eyc2ip

See Headmaster.

OKLAHOMA

http://hdmaster.com/testing/cnatesting/oklahoma/okform-pages/okforms/OKCandidateHandbook.pdf

Or use shortened URL: http://bit.ly/2bygz3I

See also Prometric; Headmaster.

OREGON

http://hdmaster.com/testing/cnatesting/oregon/orformpages/ORCandidateHandbook.pdf

Or use shortened URL: http://bit.ly/2bQPKqi

http://www.oregon.gov/osbn/pages/cnacertification.aspx

See Headmaster.

PENNSYLVANIA

http://www.education.pa.gov/K-12/Career%20and%20Technical%20Education/Nurse%20Aide%20Training%20Program/Pages/default.aspx#tab-1

Or use shortened URL: http://bit.ly/2e192bQ

Type "CNA" in search box. See also Pearson Vue and Red Cross.

RHODE ISLAND

http://www.health.ri.gov/licenses/detail.php?id=232

See also Pearson Vue.

South Carolina

https://www.scdhhs.gov/organizations/nurse-aide-registry-testing-and-training

Or use shortened URL: http://bit.ly/2bjKg9I

See also Pearson Vue.

South Dakota

https://doh.sd.gov/boards/nursing/nurseaid.aspx

See also Headmaster.

Tennessee

https://tn.gov/health/article/hcf-nurseaide

See also Headmaster.

Texas

Use search tool on new website home page.

See also Pearson Vue.

Utah

http://www.utahcna.com/

Same site as Headmaster.

Vermont

https://www.sec.state.vt.us/professional-regulation/list-of-professions/nursing/licensed-nursing-assistants.aspx#

Or use shortened URL: http://bit.ly/2bhpQPV

See also Pearson Vue; Red Cross.

VIRGINIA

https://www.dhp.virginia.gov/nursing/nursing_forms.htm#CNA

Use search tool. See also Pearson Vue.

WASHINGTON

http://www.doh.wa.gov/LicensesPermitsandCertificates/ProfessionsNewReneworUpdate/NursingAssistant

Or use shortened URL: http://bit.ly/2bBFzUB

See also Pearson Vue.

WEST VIRGINIA

https://ohflac.wv.gov/factype.html#type=NA

WISCONSIN

https://www.dhs.wisconsin.gov/caregiver/nurse-aide/natd-registry.htm

Or use shortened URL: http://bit.ly/2bpoZbM

See Also Pearson Vue; Red Cross

WYOMING

https://nursing-online.state.wy.us/Default.aspx?page=16

See also Pearson Vue; Red Cross

U.S. Territories

American Samoa

http://www.amsamoa.edu/departments/nursing.html

http://www.amsamoa.edu/academicprograms/ccnursing.html

Guam

http://www.gbne.org/Portals/2/GBNE%20Minimal%20Requirements.pdf

Northern Mariana Islands

http://www.nmicbne.com/

Puerto Rico

http://cpepr.org/ (College of Nursing Professionals in Puerto Rico)

The website is in Spanish, but you can use the Google translator to review each webpage in English (or in the your language of choice). We recommend you reach out by phone or email. For more information, you can visit their Contact Us page at http://cpepr.org/contactenos.

Virgin Islands

http://www.thevibnl.org/

TEST SERVICE COMPANIES/ STATE PARTNER WEBSITES

Prometric: https://www.prometric.com/en-us/Pages/home.aspx

Type your state in the search box or use the tab directory below by clicking the first letter of your state.

Pearson Vue: http://www.pearsonvue.com/test-taker.asp

Click the letter of your state and scroll down to find the "nurse aide" link.

American Red Cross: http://www.redcross.org/ux/take-a-class

Select CNA from the drop-down menu and type in your city and state.

Headmaster: http://hdmaster.com/

See states listed under Nurse Aide in the Licensing/Certification column.